Date _____ Address _____

Name _____

School _____

Grade/Form/Year and Age _____

When I started playing soccer _____

Who taught me soccer first _____

Now I play at _____

My coach is _____

Who assist coach _____

My coach calls me _____

Why I like my coach _____

_____

_____

My coach often tells me _____

_____

_____

_____

My coach often tells me _____

_____

_____

_____

Why I like playing soccer _____

_____

_____

_____

My goal is _____

_____

_____

My favorite teams: 1. _____
                    2. _____
                    3. _____

My favorite players: ① _____
                     ② _____
                     ③ _____

Three things I admire most about each favorite player

① -- _____
   -- _____
   -- _____

② -- _____
   -- _____
   -- _____

③ -- _____
   -- _____

The interesting things about soccer _____
_____
_____

The funny thing ever happened to me playing soccer _____
_____
_____

The bad/weird thing ever happened to me playing soccer _____
_____
_____

PRE-SEASON PRACTICE

From Monday _____ to Friday _____ How many times _____
                Date   Date

1st practice was: Very easy ☐ Easy ☐ Average ☐ Hard ☐ Very hard ☐
2nd practice was: Very easy ☐ Easy ☐ Average ☐ Hard ☐ Very hard ☐
3rd practice was: Very easy ☐ Easy ☐ Average ☐ Hard ☐ Very hard ☐

1st practice: 🙂 😐 🙁   2nd practice: 🙂 😐 🙁   3rd practice: 🙂 😐 🙁

Coach focused on _____
_____
_____
_____

I focused on _____
_____
_____

What I'v learnt _____
_____
_____

My weaknesses/strengths _____
_____
_____

Coach advice _____
_____
_____

Additional notes _____
_____
_____

PRE-SEASON PRACTICE

From Monday _____ to Friday _____ How many times _____
         Date   Date

1st practice was: Very easy ☐ Easy ☐ Average ☐ Hard ☐ Very hard ☐
2nd practice was: Very easy ☐ Easy ☐ Average ☐ Hard ☐ Very hard ☐
3rd practice was: Very easy ☐ Easy ☐ Average ☐ Hard ☐ Very hard ☐

1st practice: 🙂 😐 ☹   2nd practice: 🙂 😐 ☹   3rd practice: 🙂 😐 ☹

Coach focused on
_____
_____
_____
_____

I focused on
_____
_____
_____
_____

What I'v learnt
_____
_____
_____

My weaknesses/strengths
_____
_____
_____

Coach advice
_____
_____
_____
_____

Additional notes
_____
_____
_____

PRE-SEASON PRACTICE

From Monday _____ to Friday _____ How many times _____
              Date   Date

1st practice was: Very easy ☐ Easy ☐ Average ☐ Hard ☐ Very hard ☐
2nd practice was: Very easy ☐ Easy ☐ Average ☐ Hard ☐ Very hard ☐
3rd practice was: Very easy ☐ Easy ☐ Average ☐ Hard ☐ Very hard ☐

1st practice: 🙂 😐 ☹ 2nd practice: 🙂 😐 ☹ 3rd practice: 🙂 😐 ☹

Coach focused on
_____
_____
_____
_____

I focused on
_____
_____
_____

What I'v learnt
_____
_____
_____

My weaknesses/strengths
_____
_____
_____

Coach advice
_____
_____
_____

Additional notes
_____
_____
_____

PRE-SEASON PRACTICE

From Monday _____ to Friday _____ How many times ____
             Date   Date

1st practice was: Very easy ☐ Easy ☐ Average ☐ Hard ☐ Very hard ☐

2nd practice was: Very easy ☐ Easy ☐ Average ☐ Hard ☐ Very hard ☐

3rd practice was: Very easy ☐ Easy ☐ Average ☐ Hard ☐ Very hard ☐

1st practice: 🙂 😐 🙁   2nd practice: 🙂 😐 🙁   3rd practice: 🙂 😐 🙁

Coach focused on
_____
_____
_____
_____

I focused on
_____
_____
_____
_____

What I'v learnt
_____
_____
_____

My weaknesses/strengths
_____
_____
_____

Coach advice
_____
_____
_____
_____

Additional notes
_____
_____

PRACTICE

From Monday _____ to ⟨ Friday _____ ⟩ How many times ___
           Date   next game _____   How many times ___
                                    Date

1st practice was: Very easy ☐ Easy ☐ Average ☐ Hard ☐ Very hard ☐
2nd practice was: Very easy ☐ Easy ☐ Average ☐ Hard ☐ Very hard ☐
3rd practice was: Very easy ☐ Easy ☐ Average ☐ Hard ☐ Very hard ☐

1st practice: 🙂 😐 ☹   2nd practice: 🙂 😐 ☹   3rd practice: 🙂 😐 ☹

Coach focused on
_____
_____
_____

I focused on
_____
_____
_____

What I'v learnt
_____
_____
_____

My weaknesses/strengths
_____
_____
_____

Coach advice
_____
_____
_____

Additional notes
_____
_____
_____

PRACTICE

From Monday _____ to ⟨ Friday _____   How many times ___
             Date   next game _____   How many times ___
                               Date

1st practice was: Very easy ☐   Easy ☐   Average ☐   Hard ☐   Very hard ☐
2nd practice was: Very easy ☐   Easy ☐   Average ☐   Hard ☐   Very hard ☐
3rd practice was: Very easy ☐   Easy ☐   Average ☐   Hard ☐   Very hard ☐

1st practice: 🙂 😐 🙁   2nd practice: 🙂 😐 🙁   3rd practice: 🙂 😐 🙁

Coach focused on
_____
_____
_____

I focused on
_____
_____
_____

What I'v learnt
_____
_____
_____

My weaknesses/strengths
_____
_____
_____

Coach advice
_____
_____
_____

Additional notes
_____
_____
_____

PRACTICE

From Monday _____ to ⟨ Friday _____   How many times ___
            Date   next game _____ How many times ___
                                    Date

1st practice was: Very easy ☐ Easy ☐ Average ☐ Hard ☐ Very hard ☐
2nd practice was: Very easy ☐ Easy ☐ Average ☐ Hard ☐ Very hard ☐
3rd practice was: Very easy ☐ Easy ☐ Average ☐ Hard ☐ Very hard ☐

1st practice: 🙂 😐 ☹   2nd practice: 🙂 😐 ☹   3rd practice: 🙂 😐 ☹

Coach focused on
_____
_____
_____

I focused on
_____
_____
_____

What I'v learnt
_____
_____
_____

My weaknesses/strengths
_____
_____
_____

Coach advice
_____
_____
_____

Additional notes
_____
_____
_____

PRACTICE

From Monday _____ to ⟨ Friday _____ ⟩ How many times ___
                         Date   next game _____   How many times ___
                                              Date

1ˢᵗ practice was: Very easy ☐ Easy ☐ Average ☐ Hard ☐ Very hard ☐
2ⁿᵈ practice was: Very easy ☐ Easy ☐ Average ☐ Hard ☐ Very hard ☐
3ʳᵈ practice was: Very easy ☐ Easy ☐ Average ☐ Hard ☐ Very hard ☐

1ˢᵗ practice: 🙂 😐 🙁   2ⁿᵈ practice: 🙂 😐 🙁   3ʳᵈ practice: 🙂 😐 🙁

Coach focused on _____
_____
_____
_____

I focused on _____
_____
_____
_____

What I'v learnt _____
_____
_____
_____

My weaknesses/strengths _____
_____
_____
_____

Coach advice _____
_____
_____
_____

Additional notes _____
_____
_____

PRACTICE

From Monday _____ to ⟨ Friday _____   How many times ___
            Date   Date
                                       next game _____   How many times ___
                                                                      Date

1st practice was: Very easy ☐   Easy ☐   Average ☐   Hard ☐   Very hard ☐
2nd practice was: Very easy ☐   Easy ☐   Average ☐   Hard ☐   Very hard ☐
3rd practice was: Very easy ☐   Easy ☐   Average ☐   Hard ☐   Very hard ☐

1st practice: 🙂 😐 🙁   2nd practice: 🙂 😐 🙁   3rd practice: 🙂 😐 🙁

Coach focused on
_____
_____
_____

I focused on
_____
_____
_____

What I'v learnt
_____
_____
_____

My weaknesses/strengths
_____
_____
_____

Coach advice
_____
_____
_____

Additional notes
_____
_____
_____

PRACTICE

From Monday _____ to ⟨ Friday _____ How many times ___
                     Date   next game _____ How many times ___
                                              Date

1st practice was: Very easy ☐ Easy ☐ Average ☐ Hard ☐ Very hard ☐
2nd practice was: Very easy ☐ Easy ☐ Average ☐ Hard ☐ Very hard ☐
3rd practice was: Very easy ☐ Easy ☐ Average ☐ Hard ☐ Very hard ☐

1st practice: 🙂 😐 ☹   2nd practice: 🙂 😐 ☹   3rd practice: 🙂 😐 ☹

Coach focused on _____
_____
_____
_____

I focused on _____
_____
_____
_____

What I'v learnt _____
_____
_____

My weaknesses/strengths _____
_____
_____

Coach advice _____
_____
_____
_____

Additional notes _____
_____
_____

PRACTICE

From Monday _____ to ⟨Friday _____ / next game _____⟩   How many times ___
           Date   Date   Date   How many times ___

1st practice was: Very easy ☐ Easy ☐ Average ☐ Hard ☐ Very hard ☐
2nd practice was: Very easy ☐ Easy ☐ Average ☐ Hard ☐ Very hard ☐
3rd practice was: Very easy ☐ Easy ☐ Average ☐ Hard ☐ Very hard ☐

1st practice: 🙂 😐 ☹   2nd practice: 🙂 😐 ☹   3rd practice: 🙂 😐 ☹

Coach focused on
_____
_____
_____
_____

I focused on
_____
_____
_____

What I'v learnt
_____
_____
_____

My weaknesses/strengths
_____
_____
_____

Coach advice
_____
_____
_____

Additional notes
_____
_____
_____

PRACTICE

From Monday _____ to Friday _____ How many times ___
          Date   Date
                    next game _____ How many times ___
                              Date

1st practice was: Very easy ☐ Easy ☐ Average ☐ Hard ☐ Very hard ☐
2nd practice was: Very easy ☐ Easy ☐ Average ☐ Hard ☐ Very hard ☐
3rd practice was: Very easy ☐ Easy ☐ Average ☐ Hard ☐ Very hard ☐

1st practice: 🙂 😐 🙁   2nd practice: 🙂 😐 🙁   3rd practice: 🙂 😐 🙁

Coach focused on
_____
_____
_____
_____

I focused on
_____
_____
_____

What I'v learnt
_____
_____
_____

My weaknesses/strengths
_____
_____
_____

Coach advice
_____
_____
_____

Additional notes
_____
_____

PRACTICE

From Monday _____ to Friday _____ How many times ___
           Date   Date
              next game _____ How many times ___
                         Date

1st practice was: Very easy ☐ Easy ☐ Average ☐ Hard ☐ Very hard ☐
2nd practice was: Very easy ☐ Easy ☐ Average ☐ Hard ☐ Very hard ☐
3rd practice was: Very easy ☐ Easy ☐ Average ☐ Hard ☐ Very hard ☐

1st practice: 😊 😐 ☹   2nd practice: 😊 😐 ☹   3rd practice: 😊 😐 ☹

Coach focused on
_____
_____
_____

I focused on
_____
_____
_____

What I'v learnt
_____
_____
_____

My weaknesses/strengths
_____
_____
_____

Coach advice
_____
_____
_____

Additional notes
_____
_____
_____

PRACTICE

From Monday _____ to ⟨ Friday _____ How many times ___
                Date   next game _____ How many times ___
                                     Date

1st practice was: Very easy ☐ Easy ☐ Average ☐ Hard ☐ Very hard ☐
2nd practice was: Very easy ☐ Easy ☐ Average ☐ Hard ☐ Very hard ☐
3rd practice was: Very easy ☐ Easy ☐ Average ☐ Hard ☐ Very hard ☐

1st practice: 🙂 😐 🙁   2nd practice: 🙂 😐 🙁   3rd practice: 🙂 😐 🙁

Coach focused on
_____
_____
_____

I focused on
_____
_____
_____

What I'v learnt
_____
_____
_____

My weaknesses/strengths
_____
_____
_____

Coach advice
_____
_____
_____

Additional notes
_____
_____
_____

PRACTICE

From Monday _____ to ⟨ Friday _____ ⟩ How many times ___
             Date   next game _____   How many times ___
                                   Date

1st practice was: Very easy ☐ Easy ☐ Average ☐ Hard ☐ Very hard ☐
2nd practice was: Very easy ☐ Easy ☐ Average ☐ Hard ☐ Very hard ☐
3rd practice was: Very easy ☐ Easy ☐ Average ☐ Hard ☐ Very hard ☐

1st practice: 🙂 😐 ☹   2nd practice: 🙂 😐 ☹   3rd practice: 🙂 😐 ☹

Coach focused on
_____
_____
_____

I focused on
_____
_____
_____

What I'v learnt
_____
_____
_____

My weaknesses/strengths
_____
_____
_____

Coach advice
_____
_____
_____

Additional notes
_____
_____

PRACTICE

From Monday _____ to Friday _____ How many times ___
           Date   Date
                 next game _____ How many times ___
                            Date

1st practice was: Very easy ☐ Easy ☐ Average ☐ Hard ☐ Very hard ☐
2nd practice was: Very easy ☐ Easy ☐ Average ☐ Hard ☐ Very hard ☐
3rd practice was: Very easy ☐ Easy ☐ Average ☐ Hard ☐ Very hard ☐

1st practice: 🙂 😐 ☹   2nd practice: 🙂 😐 ☹   3rd practice: 🙂 😐 ☹

Coach focused on
_____
_____
_____

I focused on
_____
_____
_____

What I'v learnt
_____
_____
_____

My weaknesses/strengths
_____
_____
_____

Coach advice
_____
_____
_____

Additional notes
_____
_____
_____

PRACTICE

From Monday _____ to ⟨ Friday _____ How many times ___
            Date   Date
                            next game _____ How many times ___
                                      Date

1st practice was: Very easy ☐ Easy ☐ Average ☐ Hard ☐ Very hard ☐
2nd practice was: Very easy ☐ Easy ☐ Average ☐ Hard ☐ Very hard ☐
3rd practice was: Very easy ☐ Easy ☐ Average ☐ Hard ☐ Very hard ☐

1st practice: 🙂 😐 🙁 2nd practice: 🙂 😐 🙁 3rd practice: 🙂 😐 🙁

Coach focused on
_____
_____
_____

I focused on
_____
_____
_____

What I'v learnt
_____
_____
_____

My weaknesses/strengths
_____
_____
_____

Coach advice
_____
_____
_____

Additional notes
_____
_____
_____

PRACTICE

From Monday _____ to ⟨ Friday _____ How many times ___
         Date   Date
                    next game _____ How many times ___
                              Date

1st practice was: Very easy ☐ Easy ☐ Average ☐ Hard ☐ Very hard ☐
2nd practice was: Very easy ☐ Easy ☐ Average ☐ Hard ☐ Very hard ☐
3rd practice was: Very easy ☐ Easy ☐ Average ☐ Hard ☐ Very hard ☐

1st practice: 🙂 😐 ☹   2nd practice: 🙂 😐 ☹   3rd practice: 🙂 😐 ☹

Coach focused on _____
_____
_____
_____

I focused on _____
_____
_____
_____

What I'v learnt _____
_____
_____
_____

My weaknesses/strengths _____
_____
_____
_____

Coach advice _____
_____
_____
_____

Additional notes _____
_____
_____

PRACTICE

From Monday _____ to ⟨ Friday _____ ⟩ How many times ___
           Date   next game _____   How many times ___
                                   Date

1st practice was: Very easy ☐ Easy ☐ Average ☐ Hard ☐ Very hard ☐
2nd practice was: Very easy ☐ Easy ☐ Average ☐ Hard ☐ Very hard ☐
3rd practice was: Very easy ☐ Easy ☐ Average ☐ Hard ☐ Very hard ☐

1st practice: 🙂 😐 ☹   2nd practice: 🙂 😐 ☹   3rd practice: 🙂 😐 ☹

Coach focused on
_____
_____
_____

I focused on
_____
_____
_____

What I'v learnt
_____
_____
_____

My weaknesses/strengths
_____
_____
_____

Coach advice
_____
_____
_____

Additional notes
_____
_____
_____

PRACTICE

From Monday _____ to ⟨ Friday _____ How many times ___
              Date   next game _____ How many times ___
                                  Date

1st practice was: Very easy ☐ Easy ☐ Average ☐ Hard ☐ Very hard ☐
2nd practice was: Very easy ☐ Easy ☐ Average ☐ Hard ☐ Very hard ☐
3rd practice was: Very easy ☐ Easy ☐ Average ☐ Hard ☐ Very hard ☐

1st practice: 🙂 😐 ☹   2nd practice: 🙂 😐 ☹   3rd practice: 🙂 😐 ☹

Coach focused on
_____
_____
_____

I focused on
_____
_____
_____

What I'v learnt
_____
_____
_____

My weaknesses/strengths
_____
_____
_____

Coach advice
_____
_____
_____

Additional notes
_____
_____
_____

PRACTICE

From Monday _____ to ⟨ Friday _____   How many times _____
              Date   next game _____   How many times _____
                                  Date

1st practice was: Very easy ☐ Easy ☐ Average ☐ Hard ☐ Very hard ☐
2nd practice was: Very easy ☐ Easy ☐ Average ☐ Hard ☐ Very hard ☐
3rd practice was: Very easy ☐ Easy ☐ Average ☐ Hard ☐ Very hard ☐

1st practice: 🙂 😐 ☹   2nd practice: 🙂 😐 ☹   3rd practice: 🙂 😐 ☹

Coach focused on
_____
_____
_____

I focused on
_____
_____
_____

What I'v learnt
_____
_____
_____

My weaknesses/strengths
_____
_____
_____

Coach advice
_____
_____
_____

Additional notes
_____
_____
_____

PRACTICE

From Monday _____ to ⟨ Friday _____ ⟩ How many times ___
   Date   next game _____   How many times ___
                                  Date

1st practice was: Very easy ☐ Easy ☐ Average ☐ Hard ☐ Very hard ☐
2nd practice was: Very easy ☐ Easy ☐ Average ☐ Hard ☐ Very hard ☐
3rd practice was: Very easy ☐ Easy ☐ Average ☐ Hard ☐ Very hard ☐

1st practice: 🙂 😐 🙁   2nd practice: 🙂 😐 🙁   3rd practice: 🙂 😐 🙁

Coach focused on
_____
_____
_____

I focused on
_____
_____
_____

What I'v learnt
_____
_____
_____

My weaknesses/strengths
_____
_____
_____

Coach advice
_____
_____
_____

Additional notes
_____
_____
_____

PRACTICE

From Monday _____ to ⟨ Friday _____   How many times ____
           Date   Date
                  next game _____   How many times ____
                             Date

1st practice was: Very easy ☐ Easy ☐ Average ☐ Hard ☐ Very hard ☐
2nd practice was: Very easy ☐ Easy ☐ Average ☐ Hard ☐ Very hard ☐
3rd practice was: Very easy ☐ Easy ☐ Average ☐ Hard ☐ Very hard ☐

1st practice: 🙂 😐 ☹   2nd practice: 🙂 😐 ☹   3rd practice: 🙂 😐 ☹

Coach focused on _____
_____
_____
_____

I focused on _____
_____
_____
_____

What I'v learnt _____
_____
_____
_____

My weaknesses/strengths _____
_____
_____
_____

Coach advice _____
_____
_____
_____

Additional notes _____
_____
_____
_____

PRACTICE

From Monday _____ to Friday _____   How many times ___
            Date   Date
                    next game _____   How many times ___
                                Date

1ˢᵗ practice was: Very easy ☐ Easy ☐ Average ☐ Hard ☐ Very hard ☐
2ⁿᵈ practice was: Very easy ☐ Easy ☐ Average ☐ Hard ☐ Very hard ☐
3ʳᵈ practice was: Very easy ☐ Easy ☐ Average ☐ Hard ☐ Very hard ☐

1ˢᵗ practice: 🙂 😐 🙁   2ⁿᵈ practice: 🙂 😐 🙁   3ʳᵈ practice: 🙂 😐 🙁

Coach focused on
_____
_____
_____

I focused on
_____
_____
_____

What I'v learnt
_____
_____
_____

My weaknesses/strengths
_____
_____
_____

Coach advice
_____
_____
_____

Additional notes
_____
_____
_____

PRACTICE

From Monday _____ to ⟨ Friday _____   How many times ___
                 Date   next game _____   How many times ___
                                          Date

1st practice was: Very easy ☐   Easy ☐   Average ☐   Hard ☐   Very hard ☐
2nd practice was: Very easy ☐   Easy ☐   Average ☐   Hard ☐   Very hard ☐
3rd practice was: Very easy ☐   Easy ☐   Average ☐   Hard ☐   Very hard ☐

1st practice: 🙂 😐 ☹   2nd practice: 🙂 😐 ☹   3rd practice: 🙂 😐 ☹

Coach focused on _____
_____
_____
_____

I focused on _____
_____
_____
_____

What I'v learnt _____
_____
_____
_____

My weaknesses/strengths _____
_____
_____
_____

Coach advice _____
_____
_____
_____

Additional notes _____
_____
_____
_____

PRACTICE

From Monday _____ to Friday _____   How many times ___
         Date   Date
              to next game _____   How many times ___
                              Date

1st practice was: Very easy ☐ Easy ☐ Average ☐ Hard ☐ Very hard ☐
2nd practice was: Very easy ☐ Easy ☐ Average ☐ Hard ☐ Very hard ☐
3rd practice was: Very easy ☐ Easy ☐ Average ☐ Hard ☐ Very hard ☐

1st practice: 🙂 😐 🙁   2nd practice: 🙂 😐 🙁   3rd practice: 🙂 😐 🙁

Coach focused on
_____
_____
_____

I focused on
_____
_____
_____

What I'v learnt
_____
_____
_____

My weaknesses/strengths
_____
_____
_____

Coach advice
_____
_____
_____

Additional notes
_____
_____

PRACTICE

From Monday _____ to ⟨ Friday _____ How many times ___
                     Date   next game _____ How many times ___
                                         Date

1st practice was: Very easy ☐ Easy ☐ Average ☐ Hard ☐ Very hard ☐
2nd practice was: Very easy ☐ Easy ☐ Average ☐ Hard ☐ Very hard ☐
3rd practice was: Very easy ☐ Easy ☐ Average ☐ Hard ☐ Very hard ☐

1st practice: 🙂 😐 ☹   2nd practice: 🙂 😐 ☹   3rd practice: 🙂 😐 ☹

Coach focused on
_____
_____
_____

I focused on
_____
_____
_____

What I'v learnt
_____
_____
_____

My weaknesses/strengths
_____
_____
_____

Coach advice
_____
_____
_____

Additional notes
_____
_____
_____

PRACTICE

From Monday _____ to ⟨ Friday _____ How many times ___
           Date   next game _____ How many times ___
                                 Date

1st practice was: Very easy ☐ Easy ☐ Average ☐ Hard ☐ Very hard ☐
2nd practice was: Very easy ☐ Easy ☐ Average ☐ Hard ☐ Very hard ☐
3rd practice was: Very easy ☐ Easy ☐ Average ☐ Hard ☐ Very hard ☐

1st practice: 🙂 😐 ☹   2nd practice: 🙂 😐 ☹   3rd practice: 🙂 😐 ☹

Coach focused on _____
_____
_____

I focused on _____
_____
_____

What I'v learnt _____
_____
_____

My weaknesses/strengths _____
_____
_____

Coach advice _____
_____
_____

Additional notes _____
_____
_____

PRACTICE

From Monday _____ to ⟨ Friday _____   How many times ___
            Date   next game _____ How many times ___
                                  Date

1st practice was: Very easy ☐ Easy ☐ Average ☐ Hard ☐ Very hard ☐
2nd practice was: Very easy ☐ Easy ☐ Average ☐ Hard ☐ Very hard ☐
3rd practice was: Very easy ☐ Easy ☐ Average ☐ Hard ☐ Very hard ☐

1st practice: 🙂 😐 ☹   2nd practice: 🙂 😐 ☹   3rd practice: 🙂 😐 ☹

Coach focused on _____
_____
_____
_____

I focused on _____
_____
_____
_____

What I'v learnt _____
_____
_____
_____

My weaknesses/strengths _____
_____
_____
_____

Coach advice _____
_____
_____
_____

Additional notes _____
_____
_____
_____

PRACTICE

From Monday _____ to ⟨ Friday _____   How many times ___
         Date   next game _____ How many times ___
                                      Date

1st practice was: Very easy ☐ Easy ☐ Average ☐ Hard ☐ Very hard ☐
2nd practice was: Very easy ☐ Easy ☐ Average ☐ Hard ☐ Very hard ☐
3rd practice was: Very easy ☐ Easy ☐ Average ☐ Hard ☐ Very hard ☐

1st practice: 🙂 😐 ☹   2nd practice: 🙂 😐 ☹   3rd practice: 🙂 😐 ☹

Coach focused on _____
_____
_____
_____

I focused on _____
_____
_____
_____

What I'v learnt _____
_____
_____
_____

My weaknesses/strengths _____
_____
_____
_____

Coach advice _____
_____
_____
_____

Additional notes _____
_____
_____

PRACTICE

From Monday _____ to Friday _____   How many times _____
            Date   Date
              next game _____   How many times _____
                         Date

1st practice was: Very easy ☐ Easy ☐ Average ☐ Hard ☐ Very hard ☐
2nd practice was: Very easy ☐ Easy ☐ Average ☐ Hard ☐ Very hard ☐
3rd practice was: Very easy ☐ Easy ☐ Average ☐ Hard ☐ Very hard ☐

1st practice: 🙂 😐 🙁   2nd practice: 🙂 😐 🙁   3rd practice: 🙂 😐 🙁

Coach focused on _____
_____
_____
_____

I focused on _____
_____
_____
_____

What I'v learnt _____
_____
_____
_____

My weaknesses/strengths _____
_____
_____
_____

Coach advice _____
_____
_____
_____

Additional notes _____
_____
_____

PRACTICE

From Monday _____ to ⟨ Friday _____   How many times ____
             Date   Date
                          next game _____   How many times ____
                                      Date

1st practice was: Very easy ☐ Easy ☐ Average ☐ Hard ☐ Very hard ☐
2nd practice was: Very easy ☐ Easy ☐ Average ☐ Hard ☐ Very hard ☐
3rd practice was: Very easy ☐ Easy ☐ Average ☐ Hard ☐ Very hard ☐

1st practice: 🙂 😐 ☹   2nd practice: 🙂 😐 ☹   3rd practice: 🙂 😐 ☹

Coach focused on
_____
_____
_____

I focused on
_____
_____
_____

What I'v learnt
_____
_____
_____

My weaknesses/strengths
_____
_____
_____

Coach advice
_____
_____
_____

Additional notes
_____
_____
_____

PRACTICE

From Monday _____ to ⟨ Friday _____ How many times ____
              Date   next game _____ How many times ____
                                          Date

1st practice was: Very easy ☐ Easy ☐ Average ☐ Hard ☐ Very hard ☐
2nd practice was: Very easy ☐ Easy ☐ Average ☐ Hard ☐ Very hard ☐
3rd practice was: Very easy ☐ Easy ☐ Average ☐ Hard ☐ Very hard ☐

1st practice: 🙂 😐 🙁   2nd practice: 🙂 😐 🙁   3rd practice: 🙂 😐 🙁

Coach focused on
_____
_____
_____
_____

I focused on
_____
_____
_____

What I'v learnt
_____
_____
_____

My weaknesses/strengths
_____
_____
_____

Coach advice
_____
_____
_____

Additional notes
_____
_____
_____

PRACTICE

From Monday _____ to ⟨ Friday _____   How many times ___
                     Date
                     next game _____   How many times ___
                                Date

1st practice was: Very easy ☐ Easy ☐ Average ☐ Hard ☐ Very hard ☐
2nd practice was: Very easy ☐ Easy ☐ Average ☐ Hard ☐ Very hard ☐
3rd practice was: Very easy ☐ Easy ☐ Average ☐ Hard ☐ Very hard ☐

1st practice: 🙂 😐 🙁   2nd practice: 🙂 😐 🙁   3rd practice: 🙂 😐 🙁

Coach focused on
_____
_____
_____

I focused on
_____
_____
_____

What I'v learnt
_____
_____
_____

My weaknesses/strengths
_____
_____
_____

Coach advice
_____
_____
_____

Additional notes
_____
_____

PRACTICE

From Monday _____ to ⟨ Friday _____   How many times ___
              Date   Date
                         next game _____   How many times ___
                                   Date

1st practice was: Very easy ☐ Easy ☐ Average ☐ Hard ☐ Very hard ☐
2nd practice was: Very easy ☐ Easy ☐ Average ☐ Hard ☐ Very hard ☐
3rd practice was: Very easy ☐ Easy ☐ Average ☐ Hard ☐ Very hard ☐

1st practice: 🙂 😐 ☹   2nd practice: 🙂 😐 ☹   3rd practice: 🙂 😐 ☹

Coach focused on
_____
_____
_____
_____

I focused on
_____
_____
_____

What I'v learnt
_____
_____
_____

My weaknesses/strengths
_____
_____
_____

Coach advice
_____
_____
_____

Additional notes
_____
_____
_____

PRACTICE

From Monday _____ to ⟨ Friday _____   How many times ___
                    Date   next game _____   How many times ___
                                  Date

1st practice was: Very easy ☐   Easy ☐   Average ☐   Hard ☐   Very hard ☐
2nd practice was: Very easy ☐   Easy ☐   Average ☐   Hard ☐   Very hard ☐
3rd practice was: Very easy ☐   Easy ☐   Average ☐   Hard ☐   Very hard ☐

1st practice: 🙂 😐 ☹   2nd practice: 🙂 😐 ☹   3rd practice: 🙂 😐 ☹

Coach focused on
_____
_____
_____

I focused on
_____
_____
_____

What I'v learnt
_____
_____
_____

My weaknesses/strengths
_____
_____
_____

Coach advice
_____
_____
_____

Additional notes
_____
_____

PRACTICE

From Monday _____ to ⟨ Friday _____ How many times ___
            Date   next game _____ How many times ___
                                Date

1st practice was: Very easy ☐ Easy ☐ Average ☐ Hard ☐ Very hard ☐
2nd practice was: Very easy ☐ Easy ☐ Average ☐ Hard ☐ Very hard ☐
3rd practice was: Very easy ☐ Easy ☐ Average ☐ Hard ☐ Very hard ☐

1st practice: 🙂 😐 🙁   2nd practice: 🙂 😐 🙁   3rd practice: 🙂 😐 🙁

Coach focused on
_____
_____
_____
_____

I focused on
_____
_____
_____
_____

What I'v learnt
_____
_____
_____
_____

My weaknesses/strengths
_____
_____
_____
_____

Coach advice
_____
_____
_____
_____

Additional notes
_____
_____
_____

PRACTICE

From Monday _____ to ⟨ Friday _____ How many times ___
                        Date
                       next game _____ How many times ___
                                   Date

1st practice was: Very easy ☐ Easy ☐ Average ☐ Hard ☐ Very hard ☐
2nd practice was: Very easy ☐ Easy ☐ Average ☐ Hard ☐ Very hard ☐
3rd practice was: Very easy ☐ Easy ☐ Average ☐ Hard ☐ Very hard ☐

1st practice: 🙂 😐 ☹   2nd practice: 🙂 😐 ☹   3rd practice: 🙂 😐 ☹

Coach focused on
_____
_____
_____

I focused on
_____
_____
_____

What I'v learnt
_____
_____
_____

My weaknesses/strengths
_____
_____
_____

Coach advice
_____
_____
_____

Additional notes
_____
_____

PRACTICE

From Monday _____ to ⟨Friday _____ / next game _____⟩ How many times ___
(Date)   (Date)   (Date)   How many times ___

1ˢᵗ practice was: Very easy ☐ Easy ☐ Average ☐ Hard ☐ Very hard ☐
2ⁿᵈ practice was: Very easy ☐ Easy ☐ Average ☐ Hard ☐ Very hard ☐
3ʳᵈ practice was: Very easy ☐ Easy ☐ Average ☐ Hard ☐ Very hard ☐

1ˢᵗ practice: 🙂 😐 ☹   2ⁿᵈ practice: 🙂 😐 ☹   3ʳᵈ practice: 🙂 😐 ☹

Coach focused on
_____
_____
_____
_____

I focused on
_____
_____
_____
_____

What I'v learnt
_____
_____
_____

My weaknesses/strengths
_____
_____
_____

Coach advice
_____
_____
_____

Additional notes
_____
_____
_____

PRACTICE

From Monday _____ to ⟨ Friday _____ How many times _____
              Date   next game _____ How many times _____
                                     Date

1st practice was: Very easy ☐ Easy ☐ Average ☐ Hard ☐ Very hard ☐
2nd practice was: Very easy ☐ Easy ☐ Average ☐ Hard ☐ Very hard ☐
3rd practice was: Very easy ☐ Easy ☐ Average ☐ Hard ☐ Very hard ☐

1st practice: 🙂 😐 ☹   2nd practice: 🙂 😐 ☹   3rd practice: 🙂 😐 ☹

Coach focused on
_____
_____
_____
_____

I focused on
_____
_____
_____

What I'v learnt
_____
_____
_____

My weaknesses/strengths
_____
_____
_____

Coach advice
_____
_____
_____

Additional notes
_____
_____
_____

Date _____ # GAME DAY Tournament ☐

Against _____ Time _____
Score - W D L _____ 1st/2nd period score _____ /_____ Home ☐ Away ☐
Position _____ Mood before match: ☺ 😐 ☹
Match was: Very easy ☐   Easy ☐   Average ☐   Hard ☐   Very hard ☐
Evaluation of my:

- warm up _____
_____

- effort and work rate level _____
_____
_____

- speed _____
- spacing _____
_____

- decision making with the ball under pressure _____
_____
_____

Good parts of my play were _____
_____
_____
_____

What I could do better _____
_____
_____

I rate my performance today as_____
What I want to improve upon in practice _____
_____
_____

Date _____ # GAME DAY Tournament ☐

Against _____ Time _____
Score - W D L _____ 1st/2nd period score _____ /_____ Home ☐ Away ☐
Position _____ Mood before match: ☺ 😐 ☹
Match was: Very easy ☐   Easy ☐   Average ☐   Hard ☐   Very hard ☐
Evaluation of my:

   - warm up _____
_____

   - effort and work rate level _____
_____
_____

   - speed _____
   - spacing _____
_____

   - decision making with the ball under pressure_____
_____
_____

Good parts of my play were _____
_____
_____
_____

What I could do better _____
_____
_____

I rate my performance today as_____
What I want to improve upon in practice _____
_____
_____

Date _____ # GAME DAY Tournament ☐

Against _____ Time _____
Score - W D L _____ 1ˢᵗ/2ⁿᵈ period score _____ /_____ Home ☐ Away ☐
Position _____ Mood before match: ☺ 😐 ☹
Match was: Very easy ☐   Easy ☐   Average ☐   Hard ☐   Very hard ☐
Evaluation of my:

- warm up _____

_____

- effort and work rate level _____

_____
_____

- speed _____
- spacing _____

_____

- decision making with the ball under pressure _____

_____
_____

Good parts of my play were _____

_____
_____

What I could do better _____

_____
_____

I rate my performance today as _____
What I want to improve upon in practice _____

_____

Date _____ # GAME DAY Tournament ☐

Against _____ Time _____
Score - W D L _____ 1st/2nd period score _____ /_____ Home ☐ Away ☐
Position _____ Mood before match: ☺ 😐 ☹
Match was: Very easy ☐   Easy ☐   Average ☐   Hard ☐   Very hard ☐

Evaluation of my:

- warm up _____
_____

- effort and work rate level _____
_____
_____

- speed _____
- spacing _____
_____

- decision making with the ball under pressure _____
_____
_____

Good parts of my play were _____
_____
_____
_____

What I could do better _____
_____
_____

I rate my performance today as _____
What I want to improve upon in practice _____
_____
_____

Date _____ # GAME DAY Tournament ☐

Against _____ Time _____
Score - W D L _____ 1st/2nd period score _____ /_____ Home ☐ Away ☐
Position _____ Mood before match: ☺ 😐 ☹
Match was: Very easy ☐ Easy ☐ Average ☐ Hard ☐ Very hard ☐
Evaluation of my:

    - warm up _____

_____

    - effort and work rate level _____

_____
_____

    - speed _____
    - spacing _____

_____

    - decision making with the ball under pressure_____

_____
_____

Good parts of my play were _____

_____
_____

What I could do better _____

_____
_____

I rate my performance today as_____
What I want to improve upon in practice _____

_____
_____

Date _____ **GAME DAY** Tournament ☐

Against _____ Time _____
Score - W D L _____ 1st/2nd period score _____ / _____ Home ☐ Away ☐
Position _____ Mood before match: ☺ 😐 ☹
Match was: Very easy ☐ Easy ☐ Average ☐ Hard ☐ Very hard ☐
Evaluation of my:

   - warm up _____
_____

   - effort and work rate level _____
_____
_____

   - speed _____
   - spacing _____
_____

   - decision making with the ball under pressure_____
_____
_____

Good parts of my play were _____
_____
_____

What I could do better _____
_____
_____

I rate my performance today as_____
What I want to improve upon in practice _____
_____
_____

Date _____ # GAME DAY Tournament ☐

Against _____ Time _____
Score - W D L _____ 1ˢᵗ/2ⁿᵈ period score _____ / _____ Home ☐ Away ☐
Position _____ Mood before match: 😊 😐 ☹
Match was: Very easy ☐ Easy ☐ Average ☐ Hard ☐ Very hard ☐
Evaluation of my:

- warm up _____
_____

- effort and work rate level _____
_____
_____

- speed _____
- spacing _____
_____

- decision making with the ball under pressure_____
_____
_____

Good parts of my play were _____
_____
_____
_____

What I could do better _____
_____
_____

I rate my performance today as_____
What I want to improve upon in practice _____
_____
_____

Date _____ # GAME DAY Tournament ☐

Against _____ Time _____
Score - W D L _____ 1st/2nd period score _____ /_____ Home ☐ Away ☐
Position _____ Mood before match: ☺ 😐 ☹
Match was: Very easy ☐   Easy ☐   Average ☐   Hard ☐   Very hard ☐
Evaluation of my:

   - warm up _____
   _____

   - effort and work rate level _____
   _____
   _____

   - speed _____
   - spacing _____
   _____

   - decision making with the ball under pressure _____
   _____
   _____

Good parts of my play were _____
_____
_____
_____

What I could do better _____
_____
_____

I rate my performance today as_____
What I want to improve upon in practice _____
_____
_____

Date _____ # GAME DAY Tournament ☐

Against _____ Time _____
Score - W D L _____ 1st/2nd period score _____ /_____ Home ☐ Away ☐
Position _____ Mood before match: ☺ 😐 ☹
Match was: Very easy ☐   Easy ☐   Average ☐   Hard ☐   Very hard ☐
Evaluation of my:

- warm up _____
_____

- effort and work rate level _____
_____
_____

- speed _____
- spacing _____
_____

- decision making with the ball under pressure_____
_____
_____

Good parts of my play were _____
_____
_____
_____

What I could do better _____
_____
_____

I rate my performance today as_____
What I want to improve upon in practice _____
_____
_____

Date _____ **GAME DAY** Tournament ☐

Against _____ Time _____
Score - W D L _____ 1st/2nd period score _____ /_____ Home ☐ Away ☐
Position _____ Mood before match: 😊 😐 ☹
Match was: Very easy ☐   Easy ☐   Average ☐   Hard ☐   Very hard ☐
Evaluation of my:

- warm up _____
_____

- effort and work rate level _____
_____
_____

- speed _____
- spacing _____
_____

- decision making with the ball under pressure_____
_____
_____

Good parts of my play were _____
_____
_____
_____

What I could do better _____
_____
_____

I rate my performance today as_____
What I want to improve upon in practice _____
_____
_____

PRACTICE

From Monday _____ to ⟨ Friday _____ ⟩ How many times ___
              Date   next game _____   How many times ___
                                    Date

1st practice was: Very easy ☐ Easy ☐ Average ☐ Hard ☐ Very hard ☐
2nd practice was: Very easy ☐ Easy ☐ Average ☐ Hard ☐ Very hard ☐
3rd practice was: Very easy ☐ Easy ☐ Average ☐ Hard ☐ Very hard ☐

1st practice: 🙂 😐 ☹   2nd practice: 🙂 😐 ☹   3rd practice: 🙂 😐 ☹

Coach focused on _____
_____
_____
_____

I focused on _____
_____
_____
_____

What I'v learnt _____
_____
_____
_____

My weaknesses/strengths _____
_____
_____
_____

Coach advice _____
_____
_____
_____

Additional notes _____
_____
_____

Date _____   # GAME DAY   Tournament ☐

Against _____   Time _____
Score - W D L _____   1st/2nd period score _____ / _____   Home ☐ Away ☐
Position _____   Mood before match: 😊 😐 ☹
Match was: Very easy ☐   Easy ☐   Average ☐   Hard ☐   Very hard ☐
Evaluation of my:

- warm up _____
_____

- effort and work rate level _____
_____
_____

- speed _____
- spacing _____
_____

- decision making with the ball under pressure _____
_____
_____

Good parts of my play were _____
_____
_____

What I could do better _____
_____
_____

I rate my performance today as _____
What I want to improve upon in practice _____
_____
_____

GAME DAY

Date _____   Tournament ☐

Against _____ Time _____
Score - W D L _____ 1st/2nd period score _____ /_____ Home ☐ Away ☐
Position _____ Mood before match: ☺ 😐 ☹
Match was: Very easy ☐   Easy ☐   Average ☐   Hard ☐   Very hard ☐

Evaluation of my:

- warm up _____
_____

- effort and work rate level _____
_____
_____

- speed _____
- spacing _____
_____

- decision making with the ball under pressure _____
_____
_____

Good parts of my play were _____
_____
_____

What I could do better _____
_____
_____

I rate my performance today as _____
What I want to improve upon in practice _____
_____
_____

Date _____ # GAME DAY Tournament ☐

Against _____ Time _____
Score - W D L _____ 1st/2nd period score _____ / _____ Home ☐ Away ☐
Position _____ Mood before match: ☺ 😐 ☹
Match was: Very easy ☐   Easy ☐   Average ☐   Hard ☐   Very hard ☐
Evaluation of my:

- warm up _____
_____

- effort and work rate level _____
_____
_____

- speed _____
- spacing _____
_____

- decision making with the ball under pressure_____
_____
_____

Good parts of my play were _____
_____
_____
_____

What I could do better _____
_____
_____

I rate my performance today as_____
What I want to improve upon in practice _____
_____
_____

Date _____ # GAME DAY Tournament ☐

Against _____ Time _____
Score - W D L _____ 1st/2nd period score _____ / _____ Home ☐ Away ☐
Position _____ Mood before match: ☺ 😐 ☹
Match was: Very easy ☐   Easy ☐   Average ☐   Hard ☐   Very hard ☐

Evaluation of my:

- warm up _____
_____

- effort and work rate level _____
_____
_____

- speed _____
- spacing _____
_____

- decision making with the ball under pressure_____
_____
_____

Good parts of my play were _____
_____
_____
_____

What I could do better _____
_____
_____
_____

I rate my performance today as_____
What I want to improve upon in practice _____
_____

Date _____ # GAME DAY Tournament ☐

Against _____ Time _____
Score - W D L _____ 1st/2nd period score _____ / _____ Home ☐ Away ☐
Position _____ Mood before match: ☺ 😐 ☹
Match was: Very easy ☐   Easy ☐   Average ☐   Hard ☐   Very hard ☐
Evaluation of my:

   - warm up _____
_____

   - effort and work rate level _____
_____
_____

   - speed _____
   - spacing _____
_____

   - decision making with the ball under pressure_____
_____
_____

Good parts of my play were _____
_____
_____

What I could do better _____
_____
_____

I rate my performance today as_____
What I want to improve upon in practice _____
_____
_____

Date _____   # GAME DAY   Tournament ☐

Against _____ Time _____
Score - W D L _____ 1st/2nd period score _____ / _____ Home ☐ Away ☐
Position _____ Mood before match: ☺ 😐 ☹
Match was: Very easy ☐   Easy ☐   Average ☐   Hard ☐   Very hard ☐
Evaluation of my:

   - warm up _____
   _____

   - effort and work rate level _____
   _____
   _____

   - speed _____
   - spacing _____
   _____

   - decision making with the ball under pressure _____
   _____
   _____

Good parts of my play were _____
_____
_____

What I could do better _____
_____
_____

I rate my performance today as _____
What I want to improve upon in practice _____
_____
_____

Date _____ **GAME DAY** Tournament ☐

Against _____ Time _____
Score - W D L _____ 1st/2nd period score _____ /_____ Home ☐ Away ☐
Position _____ Mood before match: ☺ 😐 ☹
Match was: Very easy ☐   Easy ☐   Average ☐   Hard ☐   Very hard ☐
Evaluation of my:

- warm up _____
_____

- effort and work rate level _____
_____
_____

- speed _____
- spacing _____
_____

- decision making with the ball under pressure_____
_____
_____

Good parts of my play were _____
_____
_____
_____

What I could do better _____
_____
_____
_____

I rate my performance today as_____
What I want to improve upon in practice _____
_____
_____

Date _____ # GAME DAY Tournament ☐

Against _____ Time _____
Score - W D L _____ 1st/2nd period score _____ / _____ Home ☐ Away ☐
Position _____ Mood before match: ☺ 😐 ☹
Match was: Very easy ☐   Easy ☐   Average ☐   Hard ☐   Very hard ☐
Evaluation of my:

- warm up _____
_____

- effort and work rate level _____
_____
_____

- speed _____
- spacing _____
_____

- decision making with the ball under pressure _____
_____
_____

Good parts of my play were _____
_____
_____

What I could do better _____
_____
_____

I rate my performance today as _____
What I want to improve upon in practice _____
_____
_____

Date _____ # GAME DAY Tournament ☐

Against _____ Time _____
Score - W D L _____ 1st/2nd period score _____ /_____ Home ☐ Away ☐
Position _____ Mood before match: ☺ 😐 ☹
Match was: Very easy ☐   Easy ☐   Average ☐   Hard ☐   Very hard ☐
Evaluation of my:

   - warm up _____
_____

   - effort and work rate level _____
_____
_____

   - speed _____
   - spacing _____
_____

   - decision making with the ball under pressure_____
_____
_____

Good parts of my play were _____
_____
_____

What I could do better _____
_____
_____

I rate my performance today as_____
What I want to improve upon in practice _____
_____
_____

GAME DAY

Date _____ Tournament ☐

Against _____ Time _____
Score - W D L _____ 1st/2nd period score _____ / _____ Home ☐ Away ☐
Position _____ Mood before match: ☺ 😐 ☹
Match was: Very easy ☐ Easy ☐ Average ☐ Hard ☐ Very hard ☐

Evaluation of my:

- warm up _____
_____

- effort and work rate level _____
_____
_____

- speed _____
- spacing _____
_____

- decision making with the ball under pressure _____
_____
_____

Good parts of my play were _____
_____
_____

What I could do better _____
_____
_____

I rate my performance today as _____
What I want to improve upon in practice _____
_____
_____

PRACTICE

From Monday _____ to ⟨ Friday _____ How many times ___
           Date   next game _____ How many times ___
                                 Date

1st practice was: Very easy ☐ Easy ☐ Average ☐ Hard ☐ Very hard ☐
2nd practice was: Very easy ☐ Easy ☐ Average ☐ Hard ☐ Very hard ☐
3rd practice was: Very easy ☐ Easy ☐ Average ☐ Hard ☐ Very hard ☐

1st practice: 🙂 😐 🙁   2nd practice: 🙂 😐 🙁   3rd practice: 🙂 😐 🙁

Coach focused on
_____
_____
_____

I focused on
_____
_____
_____

What I'v learnt
_____
_____

My weaknesses/strengths
_____
_____
_____

Coach advice
_____
_____
_____

Additional notes
_____
_____
_____

Date _____ # GAME DAY Tournament ☐

Against _____ Time _____
Score - W D L _____ 1st/2nd period score _____ / _____ Home ☐ Away ☐
Position _____ Mood before match: ☺ 😐 ☹
Match was: Very easy ☐ Easy ☐ Average ☐ Hard ☐ Very hard ☐
Evaluation of my:

- warm up _____
_____

- effort and work rate level _____
_____
_____

- speed _____
- spacing _____
_____

- decision making with the ball under pressure_____
_____
_____

Good parts of my play were _____
_____
_____
_____

What I could do better _____
_____
_____

I rate my performance today as_____
What I want to improve upon in practice _____
_____
_____

GAME DAY

Date _____   Tournament ☐

Against _____ Time _____

Score - W D L _____ 1st/2nd period score _____ / _____ Home ☐ Away ☐

Position _____ Mood before match: ☺ 😐 ☹

Match was: Very easy ☐   Easy ☐   Average ☐   Hard ☐   Very hard ☐

Evaluation of my:

- warm up _____

_____

- effort and work rate level _____

_____

_____

- speed _____
- spacing _____

_____

- decision making with the ball under pressure _____

_____

_____

Good parts of my play were _____

_____

_____

_____

What I could do better _____

_____

_____

I rate my performance today as_____

What I want to improve upon in practice _____

_____

_____

Date _____ # GAME DAY Tournament ☐

Against _____ Time _____
Score - W D L _____ 1st/2nd period score _____ / _____ Home ☐ Away ☐
Position _____ Mood before match: 🙂 😐 ☹️
Match was: Very easy ☐   Easy ☐   Average ☐   Hard ☐   Very hard ☐
Evaluation of my:

- warm up _____
_____

- effort and work rate level _____
_____
_____

- speed _____
- spacing _____
_____

- decision making with the ball under pressure _____
_____
_____

Good parts of my play were _____
_____
_____
_____

What I could do better _____
_____
_____

I rate my performance today as _____
What I want to improve upon in practice _____
_____
_____

Date _____ # GAME DAY Tournament ☐

Against _____ Time _____
Score - W D L _____ 1st/2nd period score ____ / ____ Home ☐ Away ☐
Position _____ Mood before match: ☺ 😐 ☹
Match was: Very easy ☐   Easy ☐   Average ☐   Hard ☐   Very hard ☐

Evaluation of my:

- warm up _____

_____

- effort and work rate level _____

_____
_____

- speed _____
- spacing _____

_____

- decision making with the ball under pressure _____

_____

Good parts of my play were _____
_____
_____

What I could do better _____
_____
_____

I rate my performance today as _____
What I want to improve upon in practice _____
_____
_____

Date _____ # GAME DAY Tournament ☐

Against _____ Time _____
Score - W D L _____ 1st/2nd period score _____ / _____ Home ☐ Away ☐
Position _____ Mood before match: 😊 😐 ☹
Match was: Very easy ☐ Easy ☐ Average ☐ Hard ☐ Very hard ☐
Evaluation of my:

- warm up _____
_____

- effort and work rate level _____
_____
_____

- speed _____
- spacing _____
_____

- decision making with the ball under pressure _____
_____
_____

Good parts of my play were _____
_____
_____
_____

What I could do better _____
_____
_____

I rate my performance today as _____
What I want to improve upon in practice _____
_____
_____

Date _____ # GAME DAY Tournament ☐

Against _____ Time _____
Score - W D L _____ 1st/2nd period score ____ / ____ Home ☐ Away ☐
Position _____ Mood before match: 🙂 😐 ☹
Match was: Very easy ☐ Easy ☐ Average ☐ Hard ☐ Very hard ☐
Evaluation of my:

- warm up _____

- effort and work rate level _____

- speed _____
- spacing _____

- decision making with the ball under pressure_____

Good parts of my play were _____

What I could do better _____

I rate my performance today as_____
What I want to improve upon in practice _____

Date _____ # GAME DAY Tournament ☐

Against _____ Time _____
Score - W D L _____ 1st/2nd period score _____ /_____ Home ☐ Away ☐
Position _____ Mood before match: ☺ 😐 ☹
Match was: Very easy ☐   Easy ☐   Average ☐   Hard ☐   Very hard ☐
Evaluation of my:

   - warm up _____
_____

   - effort and work rate level _____
_____
_____

   - speed _____
   - spacing _____
_____

   - decision making with the ball under pressure_____
_____

Good parts of my play were _____
_____
_____

What I could do better _____
_____
_____

I rate my performance today as_____
What I want to improve upon in practice _____
_____
_____

Date _____ **GAME DAY** Tournament ☐

Against _____ Time _____
Score - W D L _____ 1st/2nd period score _____ / _____ Home ☐ Away ☐
Position _____ Mood before match: 🙂 😐 🙁
Match was: Very easy ☐ Easy ☐ Average ☐ Hard ☐ Very hard ☐

Evaluation of my:

- warm up _____
_____

- effort and work rate level _____
_____
_____

- speed _____
- spacing _____
_____

- decision making with the ball under pressure _____
_____

Good parts of my play were _____
_____
_____
_____

What I could do better _____
_____
_____

I rate my performance today as _____
What I want to improve upon in practice _____
_____
_____

Date _____ # GAME DAY Tournament ☐

Against _____ Time _____
Score - W D L _____ 1ˢᵗ/2ⁿᵈ period score _____ / _____ Home ☐ Away ☐
Position _____ Mood before match: 🙂 😐 ☹
Match was: Very easy ☐ Easy ☐ Average ☐ Hard ☐ Very hard ☐
Evaluation of my:

- warm up _____
_____

- effort and work rate level _____
_____
_____

- speed _____
- spacing _____
_____

- decision making with the ball under pressure_____
_____
_____

Good parts of my play were
_____
_____
_____

What I could do better
_____
_____

I rate my performance today as_____
What I want to improve upon in practice _____
_____
_____

Date _____ **GAME DAY** Tournament ☐

Against _____ Time _____
Score - W D L _____ 1st/2nd period score _____/_____ Home☐ Away☐
Position _____ Mood before match: ☺ 😐 ☹
Match was: Very easy☐ Easy☐ Average☐ Hard☐ Very hard☐
Evaluation of my:

- warm up _____
_____

- effort and work rate level _____
_____
_____

- speed _____
- spacing _____
_____

- decision making with the ball under pressure_____
_____

Good parts of my play were _____
_____
_____

What I could do better _____
_____
_____

I rate my performance today as_____
What I want to improve upon in practice _____
_____
_____

PRACTICE

From Monday _____ to ⟨ Friday _____   How many times ___
                           Date
                        next game _____   How many times ___
                                     Date

1st practice was: Very easy ☐ Easy ☐ Average ☐ Hard ☐ Very hard ☐
2nd practice was: Very easy ☐ Easy ☐ Average ☐ Hard ☐ Very hard ☐
3rd practice was: Very easy ☐ Easy ☐ Average ☐ Hard ☐ Very hard ☐

1st practice: 🙂 😐 🙁   2nd practice: 🙂 😐 🙁   3rd practice: 🙂 😐 🙁

Coach focused on _____
_____
_____
_____

I focused on _____
_____
_____
_____

What I'v learnt _____
_____
_____
_____

My weaknesses/strengths _____
_____
_____
_____

Coach advice _____
_____
_____
_____

Additional notes _____
_____
_____
_____

Date _____ # GAME DAY Tournament ☐

Against _____ Time _____
Score - W D L _____ 1ˢᵗ/2ⁿᵈ period score _____ /_____ Home ☐ Away ☐
Position _____ Mood before match: 🙂 😐 ☹
Match was: Very easy ☐   Easy ☐   Average ☐   Hard ☐   Very hard ☐
Evaluation of my:

- warm up _____
_____

- effort and work rate level _____
_____
_____

- speed _____
- spacing _____
_____

- decision making with the ball under pressure _____
_____
_____

Good parts of my play were _____
_____
_____
_____

What I could do better _____
_____
_____

I rate my performance today as _____
What I want to improve upon in practice _____
_____
_____

Date _____ **GAME DAY** Tournament ☐

Against _____ Time _____
Score - W D L _____ 1st/2nd period score _____ / _____ Home ☐ Away ☐
Position _____ Mood before match: ☺ 😐 ☹
Match was: Very easy ☐   Easy ☐   Average ☐   Hard ☐   Very hard ☐
Evaluation of my:

- warm up _____
_____

- effort and work rate level _____
_____
_____

- speed _____
- spacing _____
_____

- decision making with the ball under pressure _____
_____

Good parts of my play were _____
_____
_____

What I could do better _____
_____
_____

I rate my performance today as _____
What I want to improve upon in practice _____
_____
_____

Date _____ # GAME DAY Tournament ☐

Against _____ Time _____
Score - W D L _____ 1st/2nd period score _____ /_____ Home ☐ Away ☐
Position _____ Mood before match: 😊 😐 ☹
Match was: Very easy ☐   Easy ☐   Average ☐   Hard ☐   Very hard ☐
Evaluation of my:

- warm up _____
_____

- effort and work rate level _____
_____
_____

- speed _____
- spacing _____
_____

- decision making with the ball under pressure _____
_____
_____

Good parts of my play were _____
_____
_____
_____

What I could do better _____
_____
_____
_____

I rate my performance today as _____
What I want to improve upon in practice _____
_____
_____

GAME DAY

Date _____ Tournament ☐

Against _____ Time _____
Score - W D L _____ 1st/2nd period score _____ / _____ Home ☐ Away ☐
Position _____ Mood before match: ☺ 😐 ☹
Match was: Very easy ☐ Easy ☐ Average ☐ Hard ☐ Very hard ☐

Evaluation of my:

- warm up _____
_____

- effort and work rate level _____
_____
_____

- speed _____
- spacing _____
_____

- decision making with the ball under pressure _____
_____
_____

Good parts of my play were _____
_____
_____
_____

What I could do better _____
_____
_____
_____

I rate my performance today as _____

What I want to improve upon in practice _____
_____
_____

Date _____ # GAME DAY Tournament ☐

Against _____ Time _____
Score - W D L _____ 1st/2nd period score _____ / _____ Home ☐ Away ☐
Position _____ Mood before match: 🙂 😐 ☹️
Match was: Very easy ☐ Easy ☐ Average ☐ Hard ☐ Very hard ☐

Evaluation of my:

- warm up _____
_____

- effort and work rate level _____
_____
_____

- speed _____
- spacing _____
_____

- decision making with the ball under pressure_____
_____
_____

Good parts of my play were _____
_____
_____

What I could do better _____
_____
_____

I rate my performance today as_____
What I want to improve upon in practice _____
_____
_____

Date _____   # GAME DAY   Tournament ☐

Against _____ Time _____
Score - W D L _____ 1st/2nd period score _____ /_____ Home ☐ Away ☐
Position _____ Mood before match: ☺ 😐 ☹
Match was: Very easy ☐   Easy ☐   Average ☐   Hard ☐   Very hard ☐
Evaluation of my:

- warm up _____
_____

- effort and work rate level _____
_____
_____

- speed _____
- spacing _____
_____

- decision making with the ball under pressure _____
_____

Good parts of my play were _____
_____
_____

What I could do better _____
_____
_____

I rate my performance today as _____
What I want to improve upon in practice _____
_____
_____

Date _____ # GAME DAY Tournament ☐

Against _____ Time _____
Score - W D L _____ 1st/2nd period score _____ /_____ Home ☐ Away ☐
Position _____ Mood before match: 🙂 😐 ☹
Match was: Very easy ☐   Easy ☐   Average ☐   Hard ☐   Very hard ☐
Evaluation of my:

- warm up _____
_____

- effort and work rate level _____
_____
_____

- speed _____
- spacing _____
_____

- decision making with the ball under pressure_____
_____
_____

Good parts of my play were _____
_____
_____

What I could do better _____
_____
_____

I rate my performance today as_____
What I want to improve upon in practice _____
_____
_____

Date _____ **GAME DAY** Tournament ☐

Against _____ Time _____
Score - W D L _____ 1st/2nd period score _____ / _____ Home ☐ Away ☐
Position _____ Mood before match: 😊 😐 ☹
Match was: Very easy ☐ Easy ☐ Average ☐ Hard ☐ Very hard ☐
Evaluation of my:

- warm up _____
_____

- effort and work rate level _____
_____
_____

- speed _____
- spacing _____
_____

- decision making with the ball under pressure _____
_____
_____

Good parts of my play were _____
_____
_____

What I could do better _____
_____
_____

I rate my performance today as _____
What I want to improve upon in practice _____
_____
_____

Date _____   # GAME DAY   Tournament ☐

Against _____ Time _____
Score - W D L _____ 1st/2nd period score ____ / ____ Home ☐ Away ☐
Position _____ Mood before match: 🙂 😐 ☹
Match was: Very easy ☐   Easy ☐   Average ☐   Hard ☐   Very hard ☐
Evaluation of my:

   - warm up _____
_____

   - effort and work rate level _____
_____
_____

   - speed _____
   - spacing _____
_____

   - decision making with the ball under pressure _____
_____
_____

Good parts of my play were _____
_____
_____
_____

What I could do better _____
_____
_____

I rate my performance today as _____
What I want to improve upon in practice _____
_____
_____

GAME DAY

Date _____ Tournament ☐

Against _____ Time _____

Score - W D L _____ 1st/2nd period score ____ /____ Home ☐ Away ☐

Position _____ Mood before match: ☺ 😐 ☹

Match was: Very easy ☐ Easy ☐ Average ☐ Hard ☐ Very hard ☐

Evaluation of my:

- warm up _____

- effort and work rate level _____

- speed _____
- spacing _____

- decision making with the ball under pressure _____

Good parts of my play were _____

What I could do better _____

I rate my performance today as_____

What I want to improve upon in practice _____

PRACTICE

From Monday _____ to ⟨ Friday _____   How many times ___
              Date   next game _____   How many times ___
                                    Date

1st practice was: Very easy ☐ Easy ☐ Average ☐ Hard ☐ Very hard ☐
2nd practice was: Very easy ☐ Easy ☐ Average ☐ Hard ☐ Very hard ☐
3rd practice was: Very easy ☐ Easy ☐ Average ☐ Hard ☐ Very hard ☐

1st practice: 🙂 😐 ☹   2nd practice: 🙂 😐 ☹   3rd practice: 🙂 😐 ☹

Coach focused on
_____
_____
_____

I focused on
_____
_____
_____

What I'v learnt
_____
_____
_____

My weaknesses/strengths
_____
_____
_____

Coach advice
_____
_____
_____

Additional notes
_____
_____
_____

Date _____ # GAME DAY Tournament ☐

Against _____ Time _____
Score - W D L _____ 1st/2nd period score _____ /_____ Home ☐ Away ☐
Position _____ Mood before match: ☺ 😐 ☹
Match was: Very easy ☐ Easy ☐ Average ☐ Hard ☐ Very hard ☐
Evaluation of my:

   - warm up _____
_____

   - effort and work rate level _____
_____
_____

   - speed _____
   - spacing _____
_____

   - decision making with the ball under pressure_____
_____
_____

Good parts of my play were _____
_____
_____

What I could do better _____
_____
_____

I rate my performance today as_____
What I want to improve upon in practice _____
_____
_____

Date _____ **GAME DAY** Tournament ☐

Against _____ Time _____
Score - W D L _____ 1st/2nd period score ____ /____ Home ☐ Away ☐
Position _____ Mood before match: 🙂 😐 ☹️
Match was: Very easy ☐ Easy ☐ Average ☐ Hard ☐ Very hard ☐
Evaluation of my:

   - warm up _____
_____

   - effort and work rate level _____
_____
_____

   - speed _____
   - spacing _____
_____

   - decision making with the ball under pressure_____
_____
_____

Good parts of my play were _____
_____
_____

What I could do better _____
_____
_____

I rate my performance today as_____
What I want to improve upon in practice _____
_____
_____

Date _____ # GAME DAY Tournament ☐

Against _____ Time _____
Score - W D L _____ 1st/2nd period score _____ / _____ Home ☐ Away ☐
Position _____ Mood before match: ☺ 😐 ☹
Match was: Very easy ☐ Easy ☐ Average ☐ Hard ☐ Very hard ☐
Evaluation of my:

- warm up _____
_____

- effort and work rate level _____
_____
_____

- speed _____
- spacing _____
_____

- decision making with the ball under pressure _____
_____

Good parts of my play were _____
_____
_____

What I could do better _____
_____
_____

I rate my performance today as _____
What I want to improve upon in practice _____
_____
_____

Date _____ **GAME DAY** Tournament ☐

Against _____ Time _____

Score - W D L _____ 1st/2nd period score _____ /_____ Home ☐ Away ☐

Position _____ Mood before match: ☺ 😐 ☹

Match was: Very easy ☐   Easy ☐   Average ☐   Hard ☐   Very hard ☐

Evaluation of my:

    - warm up _____
_____

    - effort and work rate level _____
_____
_____

    - speed _____
    - spacing _____
_____

    - decision making with the ball under pressure_____
_____
_____

Good parts of my play were _____
_____
_____
_____

What I could do better _____
_____
_____

I rate my performance today as_____

What I want to improve upon in practice _____
_____
_____

GAME DAY

Date _____   Tournament ☐

Against _____ Time _____
Score - W D L _____ 1st/2nd period score _____ /_____ Home ☐ Away ☐
Position _____ Mood before match: ☺ 😐 ☹
Match was: Very easy ☐   Easy ☐   Average ☐   Hard ☐   Very hard ☐
Evaluation of my:

   - warm up _____
_____

   - effort and work rate level _____
_____
_____

   - speed _____
   - spacing _____
_____

   - decision making with the ball under pressure_____
_____
_____

Good parts of my play were _____
_____
_____
_____

What I could do better _____
_____
_____

I rate my performance today as_____
What I want to improve upon in practice _____
_____
_____

Date _____ # GAME DAY Tournament ☐

Against _____ Time _____
Score - W D L _____ 1st/2nd period score _____ / _____ Home ☐ Away ☐
Position _____ Mood before match: 🙂 😐 ☹
Match was: Very easy ☐ Easy ☐ Average ☐ Hard ☐ Very hard ☐
Evaluation of my:

   - warm up _____
_____

   - effort and work rate level _____
_____
_____

   - speed _____
   - spacing _____
_____

   - decision making with the ball under pressure _____
_____
_____

Good parts of my play were _____
_____
_____
_____

What I could do better _____
_____
_____

I rate my performance today as _____
What I want to improve upon in practice _____
_____
_____

Date _____ # GAME DAY Tournament ☐

Against _____ Time _____
Score - W D L _____ 1st/2nd period score _____ /_____ Home☐ Away☐
Position _____ Mood before match: ☺ 😐 ☹
Match was: Very easy☐   Easy☐   Average☐   Hard☐   Very hard☐
Evaluation of my:

    - warm up _____
_____

    - effort and work rate level _____
_____
_____

    - speed _____
    - spacing _____
_____

    - decision making with the ball under pressure_____
_____
_____

Good parts of my play were _____
_____
_____

What I could do better _____
_____
_____

I rate my performance today as_____
  What I want to improve upon in practice _____
_____
_____

Date _____ # GAME DAY Tournament ☐

Against _____ Time _____
Score - W D L _____ 1ˢᵗ/2ⁿᵈ period score _____ / _____ Home ☐ Away ☐
Position _____ Mood before match: 🙂 😐 ☹
Match was: Very easy ☐ Easy ☐ Average ☐ Hard ☐ Very hard ☐
Evaluation of my:

- warm up _____
_____

- effort and work rate level _____
_____
_____

- speed _____
- spacing _____
_____

- decision making with the ball under pressure _____
_____
_____

Good parts of my play were _____
_____
_____

What I could do better _____
_____
_____

I rate my performance today as _____
What I want to improve upon in practice _____
_____
_____

Date _____ # GAME DAY Tournament ☐

Against _____ Time _____
Score - W D L _____ 1st/2nd period score _____ /_____ Home ☐ Away ☐
Position _____ Mood before match: ☺ 😐 ☹
Match was: Very easy ☐   Easy ☐   Average ☐   Hard ☐   Very hard ☐
Evaluation of my:

- warm up _____
_____

- effort and work rate level _____
_____
_____

- speed _____
- spacing _____
_____

- decision making with the ball under pressure_____
_____
_____

Good parts of my play were _____
_____
_____

What I could do better _____
_____
_____

I rate my performance today as_____
What I want to improve upon in practice _____
_____
_____

Date _____ # GAME DAY Tournament ☐

Against _____ Time _____

Score - W D L _____ 1st/2nd period score _____ / _____ Home ☐ Away ☐

Position _____ Mood before match: ☺ 😐 ☹

Match was: Very easy ☐   Easy ☐   Average ☐   Hard ☐   Very hard ☐

Evaluation of my:

   - warm up _____

_____

   - effort and work rate level _____

_____

_____

   - speed _____
   - spacing _____

_____

   - decision making with the ball under pressure_____

_____

_____

Good parts of my play were _____

_____

_____

What I could do better _____

_____

_____

I rate my performance today as_____

What I want to improve upon in practice _____

_____

_____

PRACTICE

From Monday _____ to ⟨ Friday _____ How many times ___
     Date   Date
        next game _____ How many times ___
             Date

1st practice was: Very easy ☐   Easy ☐   Average ☐   Hard ☐   Very hard ☐

2nd practice was: Very easy ☐   Easy ☐   Average ☐   Hard ☐   Very hard ☐

3rd practice was: Very easy ☐   Easy ☐   Average ☐   Hard ☐   Very hard ☐

1st practice: 🙂 😐 ☹   2nd practice: 🙂 😐 ☹   3rd practice: 🙂 😐 ☹

Coach focused on
_____
_____
_____

I focused on
_____
_____
_____

What I'v learnt
_____
_____
_____

My weaknesses/strengths
_____
_____
_____

Coach advice
_____
_____
_____

Additional notes
_____
_____

Date _____ **GAME DAY** Tournament ☐

Against _____ Time _____

Score - W D L _____ 1ˢᵗ/2ⁿᵈ period score ____ / ____ Home ☐ Away ☐

Position _____ Mood before match: 🙂 😐 🙁

Match was: Very easy ☐   Easy ☐   Average ☐   Hard ☐   Very hard ☐

Evaluation of my:

- warm up _____

_____

- effort and work rate level _____

_____

_____

- speed _____
- spacing _____

_____

- decision making with the ball under pressure _____

_____

Good parts of my play were _____

_____

_____

What I could do better _____

_____

_____

I rate my performance today as _____

What I want to improve upon in practice _____

_____

_____

Date _____ # GAME DAY Tournament ☐

Against _____ Time _____
Score - W D L _____ 1st/2nd period score _____ / _____ Home ☐ Away ☐
Position _____ Mood before match: 🙂 😐 🙁
Match was: Very easy ☐   Easy ☐   Average ☐   Hard ☐   Very hard ☐
Evaluation of my:

- warm up _____
_____

- effort and work rate level _____
_____
_____

- speed _____
- spacing _____
_____

- decision making with the ball under pressure _____
_____
_____

Good parts of my play were _____
_____
_____
_____

What I could do better _____
_____
_____

I rate my performance today as _____
What I want to improve upon in practice _____
_____
_____

GAME DAY

Date _____   Tournament ☐

Against _____ Time _____

Score - W D L _____ 1st/2nd period score _____ /_____ Home ☐ Away ☐

Position _____ Mood before match: 😊 😐 ☹️

Match was: Very easy ☐   Easy ☐   Average ☐   Hard ☐   Very hard ☐

Evaluation of my:

- warm up _____

_____

- effort and work rate level _____

_____

_____

- speed _____
- spacing _____

_____

- decision making with the ball under pressure_____

_____

_____

Good parts of my play were _____

_____

_____

What I could do better _____

_____

_____

I rate my performance today as_____

What I want to improve upon in practice _____

_____

_____

Date _____ **GAME DAY** Tournament ☐

Against _____ Time _____

Score - W D L _____ 1st/2nd period score ____/____ Home ☐ Away ☐

Position _____ Mood before match: ☺ 😐 ☹

Match was: Very easy ☐ Easy ☐ Average ☐ Hard ☐ Very hard ☐

Evaluation of my:

- warm up _____

_____

- effort and work rate level _____

_____

_____

- speed _____
- spacing _____

_____

- decision making with the ball under pressure _____

_____

_____

Good parts of my play were _____

_____

_____

What I could do better _____

_____

_____

I rate my performance today as_____

What I want to improve upon in practice _____

_____

GAME DAY

Date _____ Tournament ☐

Against _____ Time _____

Score - W D L _____ 1st/2nd period score _____ / _____ Home ☐ Away ☐

Position _____ Mood before match: ☺ 😐 ☹

Match was: Very easy ☐   Easy ☐   Average ☐   Hard ☐   Very hard ☐

Evaluation of my:

   - warm up _____
_____

   - effort and work rate level _____
_____
_____

   - speed _____
   - spacing _____
_____

   - decision making with the ball under pressure _____
_____
_____

Good parts of my play were _____
_____
_____

What I could do better _____
_____
_____

I rate my performance today as _____

What I want to improve upon in practice _____
_____
_____

Made in United States
Orlando, FL
27 November 2024